AF270580

PETS IN THE WILD!

PARAKEETS IN THE WILD!

by Grace Hansen

Cody Koala
An Imprint of Pop!
popbooksonline.com

popbooksonline.com/parakeet

*Scanning QR codes requires a web-enabled smart device with a QR code reader app and a camera.

abdobooks.com

Published by Pop!, a division of ABDO, PO Box 398166, Minneapolis, Minnesota 55439. Copyright ©2025 by Abdo Consulting Group, Inc. International copyrights reserved in all countries. No part of this book may be reproduced in any form without written permission from the publisher. Cody Koala™ is a trademark and logo of Pop!.

Printed in the United States of America, North Mankato, Minnesota.
052024
092024

THIS BOOK CONTAINS RECYCLED MATERIALS

Cover Photo: Shutterstock Images
Interior Photos: Shutterstock Images, Getty Images
Editor: Elizabeth Andrews
Series Designer: Laura Graphenteen; Neil Klinepier

Library of Congress Control Number: 2023947472

Publisher's Cataloging-in-Publication Data
Names: Hansen, Grace, author.
Title: Parakeets in the wild! / by Grace Hansen
Description: Minneapolis, Minnesota : Pop!, 2025 | Series: Pets in the wild! | Includes online resources and index
Identifiers: ISBN 9781098246167 (lib. bdg.) | ISBN 9781098246723 (ebook)
Subjects: LCSH: Parakeets--Juvenile literature. | Wild animals--Juvenile literature. | Wild animals as pets—Juvenile literature. | Parrots--Juvenile literature. | Birds--Juvenile literature. | Birds--Behavior--Juvenile literature.
Classification: DDC 636.0887--dc23

Table of Contents

Chapter 1
Parakeets 4

Chapter 2
Wild Parakeets 8

Chapter 3
Pet Parakeets 14

Chapter 4
Caring for Parakeets 16

Making Connections 22
Glossary 23
Index 24
Online Resources 24

Parakeets

Parakeets are small- to medium-sized **species** of parrots. They live throughout the world. Australian budgerigars, also called "budgies," are common in the wild and as pets.

There are around 120 species of parakeets in the world.

Parakeets are **omnivores** that mostly eat seeds. Their diets otherwise have a wide range. Parakeets eat nuts, fruits, plants, and insects.

Chapter 2

Wild Parakeets

Budgies live throughout Australia on plains and grasslands. Budgies prefer warm, dry areas near water. Other kinds of parakeets can be found in places such as Mexico, Argentina, and India.

Where Some Wild Parakeets Live

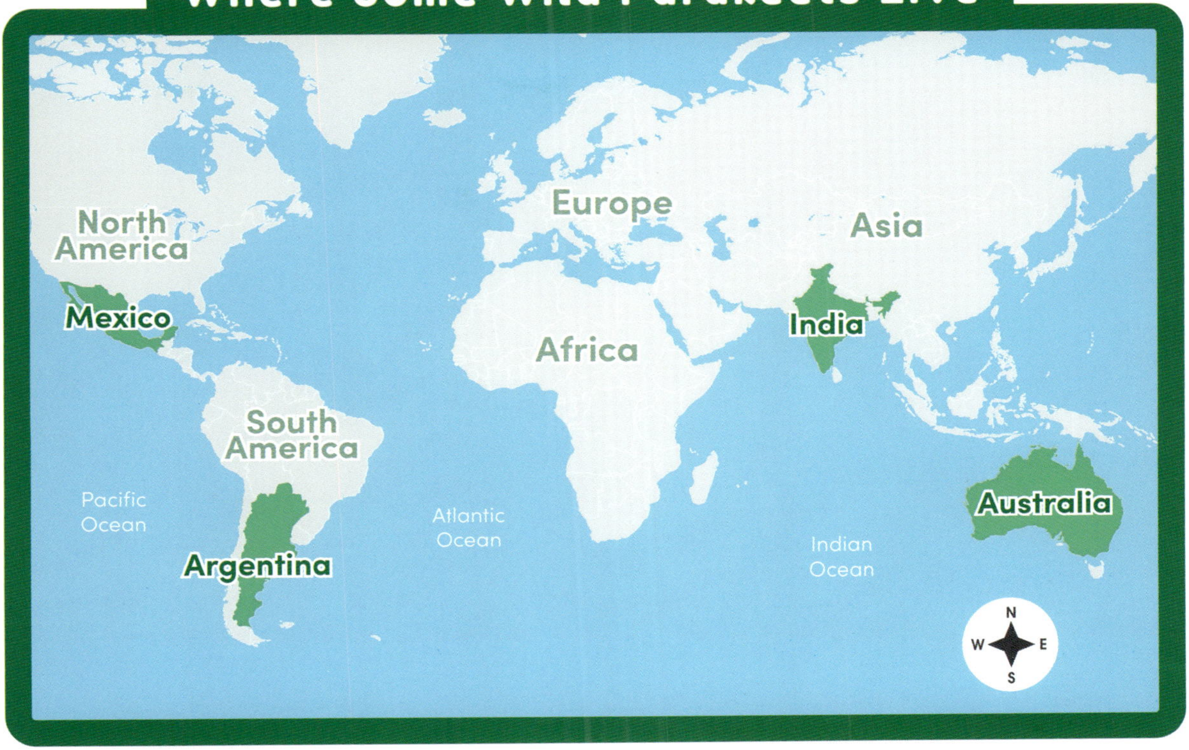

Budgies are social birds.
They are often spotted
in flocks. Flocks can have
anywhere from three to

more than 100 individuals.
Flocks fly thousands of miles
each year in search of food
and water.

Budgies also **roost** together. Their nests are hidden in tree **cavities**. Females lay four to six eggs at a time. The eggs hatch about 20 days later.

Pet Parakeets

Budgies are the most popular pet parakeets for good reason. They are beautiful, silly, and sweet. They are also smart and easy to train.

Explore links here!

Caring for Parakeets

Parakeets need a safe, clean, and roomy birdcage. The cage should have room for the bird to fly. It should also have room for several **perches**, toys, a food bowl, and fresh drinking water.

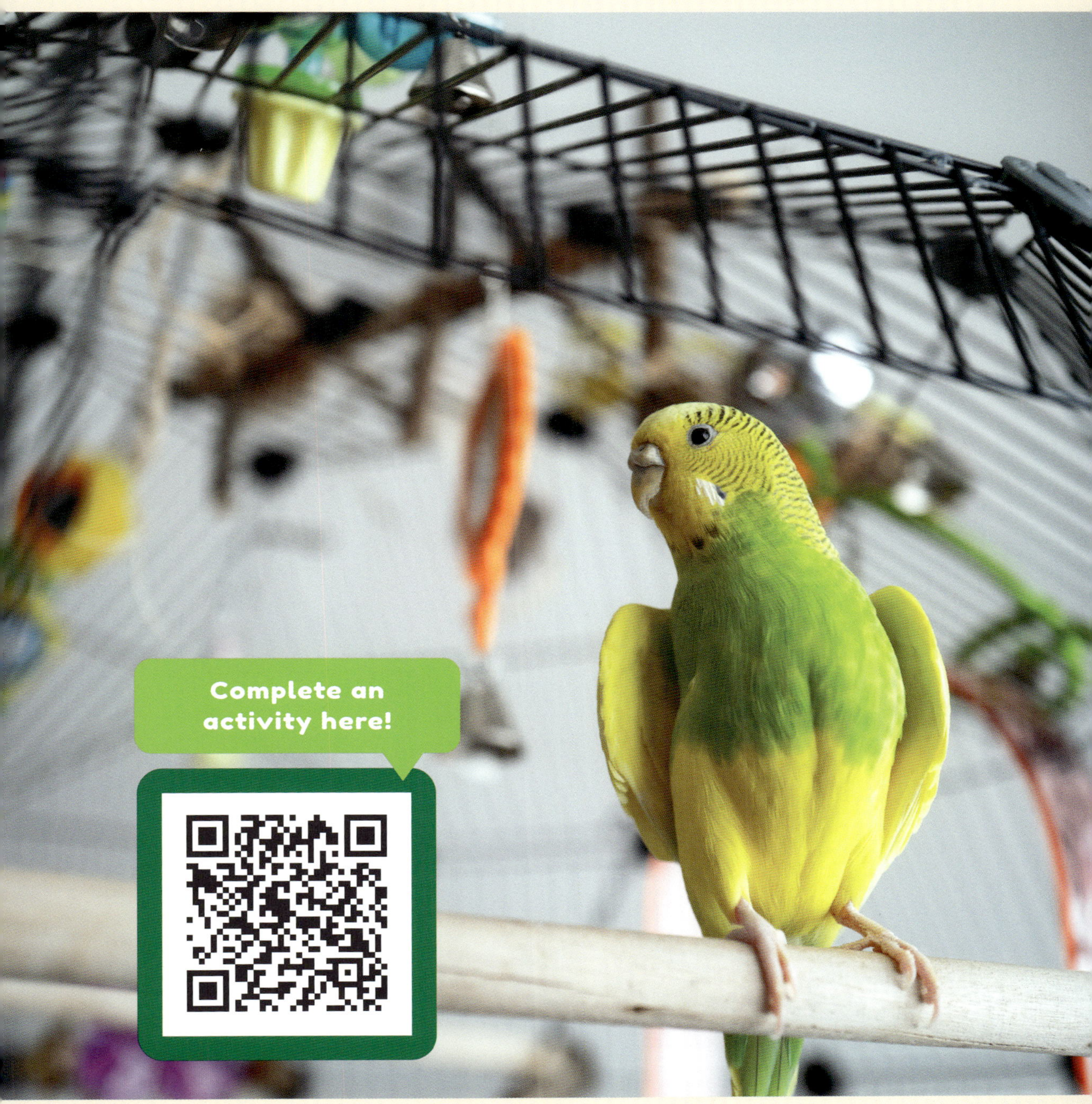
Complete an
activity here!

Windows and large mirrors should be covered when a pet bird flies in a home. Fireplaces should also be closed.

Generally, parakeets are happier with other birds. However, a human **companion** can be enough for them. It is important to spend time with a lone pet parakeet. The birds also need time to fly in a safe space outside of their cage.

Parakeets should be fed a healthy and varied diet. They can eat **pelleted** food, seeds, and certain fruits and vegetables. They do not drink much water. But fresh water should always be provided for drinking and bathing.

Making Connections

Text-to-Self

What is your favorite thing about parakeets?

Text-to-Text

Have you read any other books about parakeets? What did you learn from those books that was not in this one?

Text-to-World

There are many types of parakeets throughout the world. With an adult, look up a species that you want to learn more about. How was that parakeet different from a budgie?

Glossary

cavity – a hollowed-out space.

companion – one that keeps company with another.

omnivore – an animal that eats both plants and animals.

pelleted – formed into small round pieces.

perch – a bar or peg on which a bird can rest.

roost – to settle down to rest.

species – animals that look alike and can have young together.

Index

Australian budgerigar
  4, 8, 10, 13, 14

birdcage, 16, 19

care, 16, 19–20

eggs, 13

flocks, 10–11

food, 7, 11, 16, 20

habitat, 4, 8

habits, 10–11, 13, 19–20

nests, 13

personality, 14

Online Resources

popbooksonline.com

Thanks for reading this Cody Koala book!

This book is filled with videos, puzzles, games, and more! Scan the QR codes* while you read, or visit the website below to make this book pop.

popbooksonline.com/parakeet

*Scanning QR codes requires a web-enabled smart device with a QR code reader app and a camera.